Feathers from Heaven

a collection of poems

about life

from the heart

Angie Gillette

ISBN: 9798725980684

DEDICATED

To

Cody

for being my guardian angel

To my readers…

Feathers from Heaven is a collection of poems from the heart.

These poems are a collection of various stages in my life.

I decided to divide it into three parts. Part One is about my past with a combination of poems about the people and experiences that helped shape me into the person that I am today. Part Two is about growing up, reaching adulthood, love and loss. It's about my struggles and pain. It's about love and perseverance. Part Three is about hope. It is about the time in my life now where I have reached peace. I know myself. I still have challenges and grief, but I am able to forgive and forget, move on and help others.

Please enjoy! I hope that you can relate to them.

Life is short.

It can come and go like a feather in the wind.

~ *Shania Twain*

Hope is the thing with feathers
that perches in the soul.

~Emily Dickinson

He will
cover you
with his
feathers,
& under his wings you will find
refuge.
-Psalm 91:4
PsalmsQuotes.com

If you want to fly,
give up everything
that weighs you down.
~Buddha

CONTENTS

PART ONE- BECOMING ME

PART TWO- LIFE ROLLS ON

PART THREE- FEATHERS FROM HEAVEN

PART ONE

BECOMING ME

Becoming Me

There are many factors
that shape who we are.
Is it nature?
Is it nurture?
Is it a combination of both?

How did I become me,
The woman I am today?

Some say that I am strong,
I'm not so sure.
I know that
I am not a quitter.

I have experienced love.
Falling in love,
Butterflies,
The passion of a kiss,
Becoming a mother twice.

I have experienced loss.
Losing a friend
Cancer f*^#ing sucks,
Losing pets, loves, special things and
Family members those are hard,
Parents to a disease where they are no longer themselves,
The greatest loss of all that of my child.

I continue on with grit,
Setting goals,
Reaching them through perseverance.

A bit of a perfectionist
I may be.
OCD I am.
Honest as well.
A leader, yes.
Bossy some may say.

I have traveled and
experienced new.
Meeting people
Everywhere.

I have succeeded.
I have failed.
Regrets?
Maybe a few.
Thankful moments
MANY!

Everything
I have experienced
has played a role,
In me becoming
Me.

Just a Little Girl

Born too early one evening in July.
Just five pounds was I.

I could be held in your palm.
In a laundry basket I slept nice and calm.

Angela Marie was sweet as could be.
Always carrying her baba and her "B."

Dolls, dress-up, and playing house
Barbies, hair, nails, and make-up
Crafts and *Little House On the Prairie* books

Growing up loving to please,
Always wanting to help and appease,
Praise was frequently given,
and smiles kept me driven.

Mom

She's the one,
that gives us life.

That cares for us
no matter what.

The one who knows us best.

She's the one,
we look to for advice.

The one that worries about us often.

The one that makes sure
everything is just right.

She's the one,
that heals our wounds.

The one that tucks us in at night
no matter our age.

The one that loves
us unconditionally.

Mom

Thanks Dad

There's a special bond
between father and daughter.
It's one often unspoken.

Thanks, dad for always
making me feel safe.

Thanks for passing on
your patience and kindness to me.

Thanks for the little gifts,
Stones of granite,
kittens, and Gucci bags.

Thanks for always
supporting me.
Walking me down the aisle,
being my ice cream buddy.

See ya later alligator,
After while crocodile.

Thanks, Dad!

On The Farm

Adventures every summer
in small town South Dakota,
spent in the white
and green trimmed
Bickett farmhouse.

Times with Aunt Deb,
her soft voice and
hippie style,
An artist with a loving
heart and kindness that
always made me smile.

Pulling my dear cousins
Sheena and Sis in the
little red wagon,
such special times
I certainly treasure.

So many fond memories
running through fields
of grass and corn,
crickets and
fireflies at night,
endless dirt roads,
water towers,
grain silos,
clean laundry drying
on the line,
late night softball games,

Some memories
not so fond for me,
as silly as they may be,
skunks,
bats and rabies shots,
spinach from the garden,
roosters at the crack of dawn,
chickens pecking at my toes,
the old sow grunting at me
as I give her the daily slop,
cows on the loose,
staring into the eye
of the mean ole bull,
pretty much any animal
chasing me each day,

I love the Midwest for sure,
but a farm girl
I am not.

Hard work it is,
True dedication,
Strong work ethic,
Honest values,
It made me who I am today.

On the farm

Lake Madison

A great place to be born.
A small, quiet, little town.
Boat rides after dinner,
taking turns in the driver's seat.

Waterskiing and swimming,
sometimes in "pea" soup.
Fishing, frogs, and fireflies
Fireworks on the 4th of July.

A walk down main street
shopping quaint little stores,
time standing still,
no cares in the world.

Humid days and nights,
sitting on the little bridge
at the creek,
running from snakes
found in the field.

Staying up all night
talking and laughing,
Yelling "dibs" to sleep
in a room with no windows,
known as the "hole."

Visiting "the club,"
reminiscing days of old.
Going to the flower shop.
Great Grandma Frager,
with her chicken
and scary driving.

Lake Madison a special place
you will always be.

Parades and Fireworks

Proud to be an American,
Red,
White,
and
Blue.

Walking in the parade,
Proudly waving my flag.
Picnics,
Games,
and
Fun times.

Watching fireflies
waiting for,
Fireworks with the loudest boom,
Many traditions,
Days of youth gone by.

Rodeos,
Camping,
Fishing at the Gorge,
A boat parade,
New traditions made.
Gathering candy form the sidelines,
Jet flyovers,
Winning goldfish in the park,
9/11 patriotism reborn.

PROUD TO BE AMERICAN

Grandpa's Cigar and Grandma's Dolls

I see the water tower,
I see the water tower,
The words still ring.
in my ears.
After all these years,
the memory and feeling of honor
being the first one to say them
still remains dear.
For it meant that grandpa and
grandma's house was near.

Next, came the "dummy"
in the boat.
He looked so real,
Fishing cap, rod and reel.
Just around the corner now.

We always arrived late,
door left unlocked,
as we quietly rushed in,
I'd choose the couch to sleep,
not one wink would I muster
with the grandfather clock ticking,
chiming and an hourly dong
the whole night long.

Finally, Grandma Marie came
rolling out in her wheelchair,
early risers both are we,
time to sit and chat for hours
over coffee and plain cake donuts.

Then I would sift
through her Avon
smelling perfume and
sampling lipstick,
we would barter a bit
before settling on a price.

My purchase I would make,
with money earned from grandpa
for a stellar report card.

Over to the doll room,
I would go admiring
the hundreds of dolls.
There were dolls from
around the world,
barbies, baby dolls, and more.

Next, it was down
the many redwood stairs,
past all of the beautiful flowers,
to the lake to sit with grandpa.
As we sat on the dock,
him patting my knee
with his giant soft hands,
he would begin telling
how proud he was of me,

Hat on head,
a smile on his face,
Puffing on his cigar,
filling me in on new projects
that had been done.
That cigar a smell I will treasure.

Two great influences
in my life.
Grandpa Jack and
Grandma Marie.

Cousins

Milbank and Madison,
South Dakota strong.
Now, scattered all around
the country are we.

So many fond memories,
Swimming in the lake,
boat rides and fishing,
potlucks and barbeques,
hockey and ice skating.

Santa Claus at Christmas,
holiday togetherness,
weddings, birthdays,
funerals and graduations,
Fourth of July and fireworks,
setting grandpa's bushes
on fire.

Snakes,
steaks,
potato salad,
rhubarb pie,
and lefse
time on the farm,
bikes and wagons,

Reunions of the past
and upcoming in the future,
all grown-up,
keeping in touch,
best wishes to us all.

Love my cousins.

Pam

She may be small,
but never underestimate
her at all.
She is my longest and
dearest friend.

Many good times when we were young,
sleepovers, Shaun Cassidy,
The Monkees to name a few.

Time at the lake cabin
on the sailboat.
Bike rides to Tommy's
candy stand at the park.
Deb P.'s playhouse,
cinnamon toast, and
frosting from a can.

Then one day,
I moved away.
Visiting every now and then,
We fell out of touch,
both grown as life moved on.

Twenty years later through
Facebook each other
we stumbled upon.
Messaging back and forth
it wasn't long,
before my daughter and I
an airplane we jumped upon.

New Jersey bound with
plans of you to see,
a new friendship it would be.
Except it was as if
we were never apart.
We naturally picked-up
where we had left off,
talking, sharing, and
exploring New York
a dream come true for me.

Our visit was fun,
bagels, the best crumb cake ever,
coffee, and drinks by the pool.
A baseball game at Yankee Stadium,
Central Park, Rockefeller,
The Statue of Liberty, boat cruises,
and more.

Pam, my long lost sister
and friend,
Thanks for being you,
feisty, fun, and
always there for me.

Kick the Can

"Clankity,"
"Clank,"
the can bounces
down 7th street,
kids scatter about,
someone just kicked the can
and set us free,
run and hide again,
you only have til
the count of 10.

All of the neighborhood kids
out each summer night,
from dusk to dawn,
until we hear our parents
call our names.

Oh, how we loved
this traditional game.
We grew-up and some
moved away.

I for one could not let
this game disappear and go away.
So, when my own children
were old enough to play,
the famous game of my youth,
I taught them the sacred
neighborhood tradition,
for them to play
on Lakeview causeway.

The Old Abandoned Church

Standing in the center
of the neighborhood,
White with green shutters,
beautiful stained glass windows,
A focal point for certain,
the entire block it filled.

It sat at one end
of the square,
Leaving the rest to be
a kickball field for all to share.

Surrounded by white snowball bushes,
perfect for Barbie's.
wedding bouquet.

On rainy days,
when kickball wasn't an option,
We'd pull on the front doors
with all our might,
Carefully sneaking inside
so not to be seen,
Stepping over broken glass
while dodging birds,
the main floor we entered.

To the balcony we'd retreat,
stairs creaking and hearts beating,
Anticipation great for
the game always played….
Truth, Dare, Double Dare,
Triple Dare, Promise,
and Repeat!

It was a known fact;
the basement was HAUNTED.
I vividly remember
the bottle spinning,
pointing at me,
What was my fate?
Of course, on that rainy day it was….
Triple Dare.

Everyone's breath sucked in,
we all knew what came next,
The basement it was!

We all knew the steps
of the dare,
the unlucky person was to go
down the stairs on one side,
stand in the middle,
count to 50,
the Mississippi way,
then come up the stairs,
on the other side ALIVE.

Oh boy,
I stood at the top of the stairs
ready to faint for what seemed
like an eternity.
Staring down into my death,
I could hear sound coming from below,
creaks, moans, and groans.

The storm raged on outside,
with the wind and a crack of thunder,
Adrenaline kicked in,
I sped down the stairs,
like a bolt of lightning,
I did my counting while
peeking through fingers
covering my face,
One Mississippi - 50 done!

Over broken glass I run
and up the stairs I come.
I did it.
A hero that day,
I was for sure.

Aunt Jacque

She's a very special
person indeed.

My role model
and inspiration.

A great listener
always with a smile.

A teacher just like me.
A writer too.

I love you.
I miss you.

I'm sorry diabetes
made you the frail one.
I wish you were still here
for me to seek advice.
I hope that
I've made you proud.
My dear, sweet, and
loving Aunt Jacque.

A Teacher I Will Be

Oh, a teacher you will be.
I love school!

From my first day
of kindergarten on,
I knew what I wanted to be.
A teacher was
the goal for me.

I saved every paper
from my school days
in a giant cardboard box.

I set up classrooms
in each house we lived.

I found my students to teach,
Barbies,
Dolls,
Stuffed animals,
My brothers,
all worked hard,
some for stickers,
some for candy.

Many role models
as inspiration along the way.

I continued on the path
toward my goal.

Oh, a teacher,
I'm glad to be.

It was meant for me.

Cream Filled Long Johns

A hallmark of
my hometown.
Homemade each day
in a small bakery.

I would drive 1,000 miles
back to the Midwest,
to taste your sweet goodness.

Shaped like a bar,
more valuable to me
than gold you are.

Filled with luscious cream,
topped with white sweetness
and peanuts so fine like dust.

A childhood treasure,
I still dream of you with a sigh.

Anticipating each visit home,
to see family, friends,
and eat a long john
is true bliss
that no one can deny.

Regrets

I pick up the phone to call,
getting distracted
time and time again,
too busy is no excuse.

I don't find the time to call
then it's too late,
you are gone.

Shame on me.
A burden of guilt
forever in my gut
so strong.

I fly miles to visit
for your funeral.
Tears the whole way,
if only I had picked up
the phone that day.

Alone in your basement
wood shop I stand.
In awe of your talent
a lone picture I see,
it is of my family and me.
Tears flow heavy once again
as I ponder the years
of memories.

Oh, dear Grandpa Dale,
what a strong and
handsome man.

A quiet giant full of
kindness and integrity.
The patriarch of the family.
The glue,
always there to help
anyone in need.

Golfer, fisherman, firefighter,
and Jack's Body Shop owner.

After we lay you to rest,
alone in my hotel room,
with curtains drawn,
I'm surrounded by
old fashioned paneling,
darkness and doom,
trying to sleep,
but my mind churning,
tossing and turning
with guilt I lay.

Why had I not called
that day?
" I love you,"
out loud to you
and the room I say.
Finally, exhaustion
overcomes me.
Sleep.

Startled awake
from what I do now know.
As I sit up in my bed,
the end is all a glow.
I rub my eyes once, twice,
I see your silhouette
as plain as day standing there.
"Grandpa?" I say.

Not a word from you.
Then you are gone.
A sudden peace I feel,
no more guilt.
For you had let me know
all was well,
you understood,
I was forgiven
and now we could both
move on.

Mr. Ball

Fifth grade.
10 years old.
A great year.
A terrible year.

Mr. Ball,
My favorite teacher.
Fun.
Nice.
Blonde, curly, permed hair
70's bell-bottomed suits.

I'm not sure why
he was my favorite.
Perhaps, the memories of
how he made me feel.
I remember feeling happy
and good.
I was praised.
I had confidence.

Living in a small town my whole life.
Getting the news of
my parents uprooting me
a devastating blow.
He made me feel ok.

30 years later a Utah teacher myself.
Sitting in a conference in Philly,
I see him?!
Staring,
Stalking,
For hours I'm fixated,
I turn to my friend,
"I know him," I say.
She rolls her eyes.
He was my teacher,
I'm sure.

Awaiting in the hotel lobby
to go to dinner,
There he is again.
Still staring,
I'm positive,
It has to be,
Bald and older,
I know it is he.

We approach the door
at the same time,
I have to ask,
Yes, I was right.
Hours of reconnecting.
Facebook friends.
Small world.

Thanks, Mr. Ball.
Thanks teachers
everywhere
for building positive
relationships,
we know you care,
we will never forget you.

Sunday School

Every Sunday
Best dress
Crafts and songs
Prayers and offering

This little light of mine
I'm going to let it shine

Red, yellow, black, and white
Jesus loves the children
in his sight

This is the church
This is the steeple
Open up and see
all the people

Jesus loves me
This I know
For the Bible tells me so
Yes, Jesus loves me

Vacation Bible School
Christmas pageants
Easter lilies and bonnets

The Ten Commandments
The Lord's Prayer
Communion
The Apostle's Creed
Baptism and Confirmation
The Father, Son,
and Holy Ghost
Hallelujah
God's Peace
Growing up Lutheran
Holy, Holy, Holy
Amen

Rocky Mountains

From cornfield after cornfield
of the Midwest,
To a city a mile high,
where the mountains
are so beautiful,
almost fake to
the naked eye.

We lived atop a hill so steep,
riding your bike up
was quite a feat.
Going down was not
for the weary,
most riding the brakes
the whole way,
avoiding the crash,
no desire for
suffering defeat.

Only the brave,
were able to ride.
Free as their pedals
spun out of control,
at speeds no one
will ever know.
Heroes of the hill
we called them.

Seven bedrooms in all,
my own classroom
I set up to teach.
Our backyard was a
mountain to explore.
Rattlesnakes, caves,
and cougars.
A true adventure novel
for all to adore.

Winter in Colorado
only a year spent.
Yet, a lifetime of
scenic beauty.
Images in my mind,
remain like cement.

PART TWO

LIFE ROLLS ON

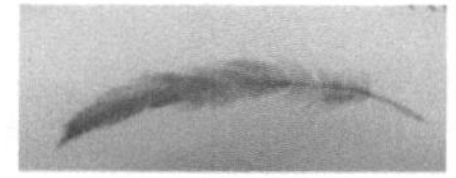

Life Rolls On

Life has brought me
a great deal of pain
and sorrow.

There have been many
dark days.
My life as I knew it
shattered by loss,
my dear son.

The days and years
to follow,
filled with heartbreak
and grief.

Surrounded by
dreadful diseases,
encompassing
those I love.
Addiction and
dementia,
I hate.
I am helpless
against their power.

Many sleepless nights
I have spent.
The ups and downs
I've underwent.
A bit useful they became,
an important part
of my grieving,
I overcame.

A time to write
at midnight,
pen to paper,
my words
would flow.

It became a time
of healing and allowed
me to spiritually grow.
A newfound faith
gave me hope.
I reflected on all of
my many blessings.
The precious moments
that have been given,
with each family member
and friend.

The signs from
my dear son
bringing me a
sense of peace.
Knowing he
is happy,
and I will
see him again.
For our time
here on earth,
is short,
just a snippet.

My profession and goals.
A future I am excited for.
I will use my talent
to help others.
I will love
with my whole heart.
I will live life
to the fullest
and take risks,
because when life is hard
you keep going.

Life Rolls On.

Just an Outsider Trying to Fit In

I moved to Utah in
junior high,
just a young
teenager was I.

As if those years
aren't hard enough,
being an outsider
was tough.

I made new friends,
but I couldn't quite
find my niche.
I bounced from
one group to another,
trying to understand
this new culture.

From the Midwest,
then Colorado for a year,
this new place was
really unclear.
I was an outsider
trying to fit in.

My accent sounded funny.
A creek was now a crick,
and warsh was wash.
Nobody knew what a
Lutheran was.

Everyone was Mormon/LDS.
One time by mistake
I said LSD,
No room for stupidity,
even if accidentally,
like wearing thin straps
on my cute dress,
to this thing called
a stake dance.

Though the looks were of shock,
I eventually learned
how to navigate and walk,
head held high
able to fit in
with relief and a sigh.

Now, I know how to fit in
anywhere I go.
As an adult I realize and know,
people are just fearful of the
unknown and new,
until they get to know you.
The secret is key,
I will just be me!

I love people!
I will always fit in.

Shy No More

Once there was a girl,
too shy to raise her hand.
Many worries,
ulcers at age eight,
silent and a follower,
always doing what
she was told.
"Being a good girl."

High School
a time to become
your own.

Jocks,
Cheerleaders,
Stoners,
Nerds,
Class Officers,
Goodie Goods,
Cowboys,
Whatever the group,
I mingled with
them all.

I see people for people.
No judgment from me.
I talk to them all.

Just do it.
I decide one day,
run for office
to be a leader.
VP I become.
People look to me
for advice.
Not afraid to speak -up,
I voice my opinion.

Adulthood.
I continue to lead
in career, family,
and life.

A leader of groups,
A leader of a school,
making speeches,
making changes,
making a difference.

Being brave.

Shy no more.

Goals and Grit

I'm no quitter,
never have been,
it's not in me.
Dedication
and
Commitment.

A job, a promise, a vow,
you have my word.
It will be done,
some way,
somehow.

Is it a flaw or a gift?
I can work under pressure,
problem-solve, and
persevere.
Sometimes I may fail,
but I will learn and prevail.

That resilience keeps me going.
I knew what I wanted
from a young age.
Set my goals,
and kept on my path.

Life have thrown
many curve balls.
Positive thinking
keeps me going.

Goals

Love at First Sight

We met at a party.
Common friends,
who knew?

From across the room
our eyes met.
Locked in a moment
of electricity I'll never forget.

We look away,
both shy that day.
Neither brave enough
to speak.
Still our glances
we did sneak.

We left the party,
each going a separate way.
By coincidence running into
each other the next day.
Both began quizzing
our friend about the other.
Finally, one thing
leads to another,
and a date was the plan.

We went to dinner
and a movie.
A gentleman you were
walking me to the door.
That first kiss
and you had me
forever more.

April Fools

We met on Valentine's Day.
it was love at first sight.
Yes, it sounds so cliché.
After our first date,
for three months we were
inseparable.
Meant to be together,
it was fate.

We talked.
We laughed.
Our relationship grew.
We had fun.
We were best friends and lovers too.
We planned our future.
We knew.

Then one night in April,
you asked me
to be your wife.
Yes, it was fast,
but with no hesitation,
I accepted.
As we told my mother
with nervousness and glee,
She responded with…
"Is this an April Fool's Day
joke on me?"

It was no joke, and
no fools were we.
We married in July
all those years ago.

Becoming a Mom

I waited and waited
for the day to come.
My dream come true.
I never knew how much
love I could feel,
until I met both of you.

A special bond between
mother and child.
So strong,
unbreakable,
and beguiled.

You are the most
precious gifts from God.
A wish fulfilled.
I promise to do my best.
I will give you my
unconditional love.

Becoming a mom
is the greatest joy.

Best Job Ever

I go to work each day,
a smile upon my face.
A feeling of joy and excitement,
even with the stressful,
hectic pace.

A principal of a school
I am.
It's the best job ever.
I am the instructional leader.
Teaching and learning
are my passion.
My priority is students,
building relationships
with compassion.

Influencing and educating.
Caring, listening, and sharing
are all part of my daily routine.

Kids say the
funniest things.
Their faces light up
when the spark of
knowledge ignites.
There's no place better
than leading a school.

Being surrounded by
our future is the
best job ever.

Surrounded by Addiction

It's a horrible disease,
taking over your life.

Tobacco, alcohol, and drugs,
the choices of my loved ones.

My dad,
my mom,
my brother,
my love,
my son,
are all the ones.

I often wonder why
some people can
give things a try,
then some continue to use
unable to quit,
while others give it up
without hesitation or fit.

The horrible cycle of abuse,
I believe it is a
predetermined fate.
A genetic trait.

Yes, it's originally their choice,
but whether legal or illegal
the substance,
for some the change
in the brain is so strong,
as addiction sets in
the deal with the devil
has already been made.
Their body is under attack
and there's no turning back.

Try as they may,
they will not quit.
No one wants to suffer
and loose everything.

I want to believe.
I try to understand,
but time and time again
they all choose their addiction
over me.
I am not enough.

I am surrounded by
many with this struggle.
I can't help but think
it must be my fault.
No, that's just silly.
Even though I try
to help, but fail.
I will continue
on my plight,
until either they
or addiction
win the fight.

Friends

Friends from the past
Friends here and now
Friends for a brief moment
Friends forever

No matter which type
Their influence on
your life will never end

Laughs, smiles, fun, and good times
Memories with friends we will always treasure
Tears, fights, and hard times
support from friends is a need beyond measure

A true friend will
always be there for you
no matter what

Friends
Badass
Beautiful
Best

A bond forever

Friends

Badass

Yes, we are!

Beautiful
Strong
Brave

Outspoken
Leaders
Attention we crave

Daring
Caring
Sharing

Fun
Loving
Spirited

Committed
Always there
Genuine

Trusting
Supportive
Dear

Friends
Moms
Caretakers

Dreamers
Goal setters
Go getters

BFFs
Soul Sisters
B*#@^+%

Brothers

The first born I am.
The only girl.
Having two brothers
instead of a sister
isn't quite the same.

Not having the same
interests can be lame.
I can be bossy, and
I know how to bribe.
Dressing Aric up to play
fashion runway
was a great vibe.

Of course, with Aaron
and Aric both as my
real live students,
school I did teach.
With a classroom in the
garage or basement,
assignments and homework
they did complete.
With my saved Halloween
or Easter candy
for their treat.

Brothers aren't so bad.
In fact, for my two brothers,
I am glad.
Mine are the best.
I am certainly blessed.

33 Years

From the moment we saw each other we knew.
A vow a short time later we were ready to take.

Married at a young age.
It's now been more than half of our lives.

Still, I wonder,
where has the time gone?
Through the years,
we've had trials and tears.
We have overcome obstacles
and fears.

There has been passion
and fun.
Now, a new phase
in our life has begun.
An empty nest
we shall soon have.

With many dreams
still to come true.
There's no one else
I'd rather spend
the rest of my years with
than you.

Sleepless Nights

Toss and turn.
Try as I might,
for there's no sleep
again tonight.
As I get up at odd hours
to write,
my angel numbers on the clock each time I see.
Letting me know my angel is beside me.

I keep going and stay strong,
writing all night long.
Telling my story.
Healing my heart.
Putting my mind at ease.

Sleep will come,
when my job is done.
Pen to paper,
my mission is clear.
Let my thoughts pour on out.

While down my face
many tears flow.
My heart still manages
to glow.

For the words on the page,
help ease my restless
mental stage.
I write until my thoughts
dry out and exhaustion
sets in.

Then quietly turn the bedroom door handle,
tip-toeing to the bed
and falling in.
Sleep at last.

The Silent Killer

I sit across from you
as you ask me for the countless time,
What is your
middle name?

You speak of days
in your past
remembering so clear,
but yesterday's events
are all unclear.

Did you eat, take your pills,
change your clothes,
or shower?
The answer is always yes.
Though sometimes innocent,
sometimes a purposeful lie
a fit you will throw.
It reminds me of parenting my own children,
but you are seventy-five I know.

Don't worry mom and dad,
I will help you as
you once helped me.
Our roles now in reverse
due to this disease's curse.

Dementia,
Alzheimer's,
so many types and stages,
none the same,
all of them awful,
to me the official name or diagnosis does not matter.
It's a silent killer
with no cure soon enough
in sight.

The time has come
where I can no longer
give you care at home
on my own.

I am
so
so
so
sorry!
Please forgive me.
I know you are mad.
I know you are sad.

I tried my best.
The day I took you to an assisted place to live,
as your eyes filled with tears,
my heart broke in pieces.
I've lived my whole life
trying to make you proud.
Never wanting to disappoint.
Now, I feel I have failed.

If one good thing comes from the silent killer,

I hope it's you forgetting your pain and sorrow.
I will always hate this disease.
I will always love you my dear father and mother.

Buddy Holly

Ricky D
You are a VIP!
With your best friend Buddy,
Everyday you'll ***Rave On.***
Oh boy!

You and Buddy have
important things to do…
concerts, golf tournaments
with Tiger, and perhaps
some events with ***Peggy Sue.***
Oh, how I wish these
were true.

I guess for you with
your diseased and
shrinking brain,
you live the joy of
planning them each
day over and over.
I'm glad that your
dementia lets you
dream and plan.
So, to you it all
seems real.

For me it breaks
my heart.
Ricky D,
keep ***Crying, Waiting,***
and Hoping, for
these things to be true.
Maybe Baby, someday
soon they will be for you.
One day you and I
will meet Buddy,
That'll be the Day
when I die.

The Darkest Day

The first day of March,
definitely not a lucky day.
At 1:30 AM my life
was shattered.

I found you dead
in your bedroom,
face down in
a fetal position.

Letting out an
earth-shattering scream,
awakening all.
No, it wasn't just
a dream.

A vision cemented
forever in our minds.
A constant sorrow
always on rewind.

The darkest day in
all of our lives for sure.
Still struggling to find
a way to endure.

Tattoos

Art
Symbols of honor
and devotion
Remembrance
Love

An integral part
of some cultures
Forbidden in others

Some planned on purpose
Some a mistake
Some on a dare

Permanent yet removeable
An individual expression
A way of standing out
Each one unique

Sharp needles
pricking your skin
Each tiny poke
full of pain as it goes in
Minuscule droplets of blood
A short time to heal

Some stop at one
Some never stop
Pleasure from endorphins
Sleeves and whole bodies
Some with ashes
Some with color
Some with words
to never forget

Millennials

Some say they are ~
spoiled
entitled
quitters
lazy
selfish
they want it all
no work ethic
freeloaders

Perhaps~
we raised them that way,
or it could be them
growing up with
technology.

I love millennials
here's why~
We've taught them right~
Maybe everyone getting a trophy
lead to them being accepting
of all others.

I love listening to my daughter
and her friends,
This is what I see…
more understanding
and empathy,
Gay, lesbian, bi, trans,
or straight
Okay, whatever.

Black, Asian, Hispanic,
White, or any other race
Ok, whatever.
They don't see color,
race, or gender.
They see people.

They are into politics and religion,
but are free
to have their own
beliefs and opinions.

Goals ~
they have them.

Millennials

Esmerelda

Mera for short,
She always gives
her support.

She calls me mother.
We love one another.

She is so sweet.
Her kindness cannot
be beat.

Her smile and laugh
are contagious.
Her lit enthusiasm
is outrageous.

My other daughter for sure.
Her heart is pure.

Love Gone Cold

Can love change?
What happened?
This is strange?

Love can change,
as our lives rearrange.

Less fun.
Too much work to be done.

Days full of grief and sorrow
with no hope for tomorrow.

The flame has gone dim.
The passion a bit grim.

From love at first sight,
to a relationship of blight.

Has our love gone cold?
Is it because we are old?

Oh, what can we do,
to help our love renew?

Hole In One

The apple of her father's eye,
She has skills nobody can deny.

Her drives go long and far.
She is familiar with scoring a par.

Her short game,
sure, is not lame.

She can read the green
and sink the putt.

With championships and
a hole in one under her belt,
her golf game is lit.
Do not underestimate her one bit.

KG you have made us proud!

Grand dogs

I have two,
each with a unique personality.

Avery,
I'm so glad we rescued you.
What and obedient loving dog you've been.

A friend to talk to when nobody is around.
Only a few mishaps with separation anxiety.
So willing to play dress-up and pose for pictures.
Now, you are old and tired and can't wait for
bedtime to begin.

Gracie,
Full of spunk and joy, you are smart indeed.
A silver lab is your breed.

A hunter and retriever
for sure.
You love your mom and toys.
The way you rest your head on grandpa's arm
staring deep into his eyes
using your charm,
It is priceless to see.
You have him trained.
He will get up and answer to your every need,
Yes, indeed.

You are both our
little buddies,
following us all around.
Our true watch dogs
barking when danger is near.
Listening for the
garage door to open,
waiting to lick us as we enter.

Being a Writer

Pen to paper,
Finger to key.

So many ideas in my head,
Waiting to be read.

Words from the heart,
Writing is an art.

Stories, poems, and information,
biographies, romance, and fiction.

Thoughts flowing,
Ideas on-going.

An occasional writer's block,
Thoughts at a standstill,
waiting for my brain to unlock.

Words on paper
help me heal,
Honoring my son,
completing a work.
with zeal.

Pen to paper,
Finger to key.

Life Rolls On

You will have dark times,
Days filled with pain,
Life sucks.
Grieve,
Mourn,
and move on.
Live your life.
Accomplish your goals.
Take risks.
Stay Positive.
You got this.
Be kind.
Be your best self.
Life Rolls On

PART THREE

FEATHERS FROM HEAVEN

You Are My Cody

I love my Cody
Yes, I do!

I love my Cody
With his eyes so blue.

I love my Cody
Yes, I do!

I love my Cody
With his cute smile too.

I love my Cody
Yes, I do!

I love my Cody
I will always be here for you!

I love my Cody
Yes, I do!

When Feathers Appear

My days are dark,
As the loss of you has
Left me with no Spark.

I've shed many tears,
As I think of our times
Throughout the past years.

I feel so alone and,
Full of sorrow.
I am no longer
Able to dream of tomorrow.

Oh how I long to see,
Your face.
I wish for one more
Embrace.

Then one day I see,
A feather appear.
It is a sight that
You are near.

A true sign of hope,
Now, I am able to cope.

For I know that you
Are always by my side.
I am happy to have you
As my guide.

Until I see you again,
My heart will always feel warm,
And my love for you will never cease.
With my mind at ease,
Knowing you are at peace.

When feathers appear.

My Beautiful Boy

When God blessed me
With a baby boy,
Oh, what a joy!
My beautiful boy!

I had waited for so long,
While trying to stay strong.
My beautiful boy!

You were perfect in every way.
My love for you grew each day.
My beautiful boy!

A teacher and leader to all,
A sportsman, hunter, and best fisherman of y'all.
My beautiful boy!

Too great for this earth to stay,
God too you too soon one day.
My beautiful boy.

Now, you are free of pain and sorrow.
You keep sending me signs and feathers in the morrow.
My beautiful boy!

A Feather a Day

A feather here,
A feather there.

A feather a day,
Keeps my pain at bay.

A feather a day,
In my sight,
Keeps my spirits bright.

A feather a day,
Helps me to know you are near.
I collect each feather and hold it dear.

A feather a day,
Oh, what a great sight.
They make my heart light.

A feather a day,
Each one a treasure.
So many signs and gifts to measure.

A feather a day,
Will never be taken for granted.
They have me totally enchanted.

A feather a day,
From my sweet angel above.
I will never forget our unconditional love.

A feather here,
A feather there.

She is Strong

Amazing, beautiful, and smart.
She has my whole heart.

Brave, courageous, and a good mind.
She is one of a kind.

Independent, athletic, and fun.
She will never be outdone.

Loud, lit, and a bit sassy.
She will still always be classy.

Patient, dedicated, and never a whine.
She's determined to keep it real and always shine.

She is my daughter.
My angel on earth.

She is strong.

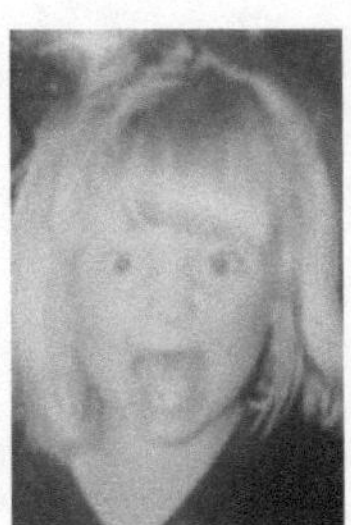

Feathers From Heaven

My angel is up above,
He sends me signs of his love.

A sign from my dear child,
A boy from the wild.

I remember when the first tiny feather
appeared and gave me hope.
I knew then I could cope.

Feathers from Heaven each day,
Relieving my sorrow, they guide my way.

I never know when they will appear,
When they do, I hold each one dear.

Feathers from Heaven fill me with gratefulness,
A yellow one appears reminding me of your playfulness.

In the wilderness you did roam,
Now, you have a different home.

Feathers from Heaven each day,
Keep faithfulness alive in the gray.

When fishing on the clear blue lake,
I see sparkles reminding me
of your eyes make no mistake.

Feathers from Heaven,
my love will never cease,
A blue feather,
I know you are at peace.

Feathers from Heaven in a purple shade,
Our spiritual connection will never fade.

Do not worry dear angel
for the pain your family is trying to deal,
with feathers we heal.

Feathers from Heaven keep us strong,
So many brown feathers keep us enduring
and we move along.

Our Greatest Gift

Children are life's best treasure,
the joy of holding them that in your arms
is beyond measure.

Their sweet smell,
makes one's heart swell.

Their passion and excitement
to learn and explore,
are traits nobody can ignore.

They walk,
They talk,
They smile,
They are amazing
all the while.

Slow down and take time,
to spend every moment with a child,
is to live life at its prime.

Yes, cherish God's greatest gift,
the time spent with a child
of any age will certainly
make your spirits lift.

Mountains

Beautiful and bold
that's what I see
as I look at the
majestic mountains
that surround me.

On this day
they sparkle and shine
all snowcapped
glistening with
white powder
so fine.

I marvel at their sight
whether day or night
they welcome us all
to climb and explore
with open arms
but make no mistake
nor be fooled
by mother nature's charms
for she can change
in a minute
to inflict harm.

Still man and species alike
will continue to hike
these incredible landforms of old
admiring their beauty
that makes them bold.

Wildboy

Full of adventure and life
from the time you could walk,
always wanting to explore.
Spending time in
the great outdoors.

Hunting, fishing, trapping,
hiking and many more.

Your knowledge and expertise
are not for us to ignore.

You guide and teach many
for that they thank and praise you,
the great mentor.

Your smile, talent, and
physical ability
we all adore.

From the fish releasing routine,
to the mountain goat climbing,
we will forever enjoy memories galore.

RIP
Utah Wildboy
C.G.

Fishing With My Best Friend

Here fishy, fishy…
From a young age we all knew,
fishing was your passion
something you were born to do.

On the banks of Stansbury Lake,
with a stick as a pole
some used line with a bare hook,
you fish away while
your sissy is at lessons.

Then I hear…
"Mom, I got one,"
as you proudly come running
fish on display.
Caught on bare hook and all.
I knew you had a gift
right then and there.

As you grew,
your love for fishing grew.
Strawberry Reservoir, Flaming Gorge,
Jordanelle, Lake Powell
to name a few.

Fishing with your
best friend dad
was all you both
wanted to do.

Let's not forget the trip to
Madison Lake in South Dakota,
where a giant carp made you
king of the day,
with cousins following
all in awe.

Bass Master, Crappie King,
and
Fishing Legend.

No-Hitter

People in the stands all around,
Majestically he takes the mound.

Watching as a nervous mom,
My heart ticking like a bomb.

Batter-up for the pitch,
It's strike after strike as the pitcher has found his niche.

Batter after Batter,
The stands and bench full of chatter.

A look at the scoreboard,
Everyone knows the possibility of what's happening
Cannot be ignored.

The pitcher sits alone in solace,
Channeling his focus on how to keep the game flawless.

As the moment comes for the final showdown,
He knows his team will not let him down.

The crowd once full of chatter,
Now silent as the wait for the duel between pitcher and batter.

The mother on the edge of her seat,
Closes her eyes though peeking at each pitch
anticipating the outcome of her son's amazing feat.

As the final pitch is thrown,
Ball lingering in the air,
As the victor is not yet known.

Strike! Batter Out!
People scream and shout!
They charge the field and
Raise him high.

A proud mom in the stands lets out a sigh,
With a tear in her eye.

A Mother's Love

There is nothing stronger.
There is nothing that lasts longer.

The love of a mother
is like no other.

From the moment of
conception, it grows.
It never slows.

An unbreakable bond.
A mother of her child
is forever fond.

From the first time holding
baby in her arm.
She promises that nobody
will do her sweet child any harm.

So many hopes and dreams.
As her child makes
her proud, she beams.

Love unconditional and true,
A mother's love always with you.

THE LITTLE THINGS

Life is short this I know,
Enjoy the little things
before you go.

The smell of a baby
as you kiss,
her chubby cheeks.

That first kiss
with the one you love
gives you butterflies
for weeks.

Reading a good book,
Delicious food prepared
by a good cook.

Watching others faces
light up with smiles.
Traveling the world
for miles and miles.

The look and feel
of shoes.
Having the freedom
to choose.

The sound and smell
of the ocean, waves,
and rain.
The majestic mountains
as they reign.

The beauty of glistening
fresh fallen snow.
Sitting by a warm fire
all a glow.

The sound of
a child's giggle.
The never-ending
of a puppy's wiggle.

The excitement of
a child on Christmas.
The first sip of coffee
in the morning-pure bliss.

Endless stories from
grandparents and
our elders so wise.
Enjoy the little things,
they are truly a special prize.

Healing

That terrible night,
my heart shattered
as I screamed your name!
Will I ever be the same?

You were gone to soon,
I hate that needle
and spoon.

Why did I not go to you sooner and check?
Now, I am a total wreck.

How will I survive?
I have absolutely no drive!

Then I take time to gaze.
The family and friends
all around me are left
in a haze.

I try to sleep each night.
Instead with insomnia as my new plight,
I decide to write.

You came to me
as I lay in bed.
Your voice I clearly
heard in my head.

"Mom, I'm okay,"
you say.
"It was an accident
that day."
"You had to find me, cuz
you are strong I see."
"I promise I really
wanted to stay."
"God just didn't see it
the same way."

"Now it's up to you to
rise up and be strong."
"You are the one to help
the others along."

"Healing will be hard
and never fully come,
but do your best and
do not to anger nor
to sorrow succumb."

Son, I know you are with me
at my side.
Hope, Peace, and Healing
you provide.

Memories

The most important
things to hold dear,
special times
with family and friends
every year.

A snapshot in my mind.
The unforgettable
times with you
they remind.

For those who
have passed,
I'm thankful
our memories will
outlast.

For friends no longer here,
Our memories I hold dear.

Memories what a
precious gift.
May they continue to
give our hearts a lift.

My memories of you,
my dear son,
are a treasure.
To see your face
and hear your voice
through thoughts,
pictures, and video
is a blessing
beyond measure.
Memories keeping you alive,
giving me
hope and drive.

Enjoy Every Moment

Slow down
Stop
Stare
Listen

Enjoy Every Moment

Visit a friend
Call a relative
Sing at the top of your lungs
Dance

Enjoy Every Moment

Buy the shoes
Get the handbag too
Take the trip
Post the pics

Enjoy every moment

Go for a walk
Meditate
Go to the spa
Eat the dessert

Enjoy Every Moment

Climb that mountain
Ride that bull
Skydive
Go skinny-dipping

Enjoy Every Moment

Get lost in a book
Lay on the beach
Watch funny movies
Sit and do nothing

Enjoy Every Moment

Smile at a stranger
Pay it forward
Be kind always
Go to church

Enjoy Every Moment
Tell people you love them
Say hi
Do that thing now
Never take life for granted

Enjoy Every Moment

God's Plan

Why
Why
Why

Why did you do that to me?
It hurts so bad can't you see?
I'm angry and full of hate.
I'm desolate.

Why
Why
Why

My son is gone.
My friend is gone.
My family members gone.
Why
Why
Why

Wait…
I understand.
It's your plan.
It was in place before
my life began.

Why
Why
Why

I have thought long and through prayer I now trust.
My attitude I will adjust.

Why
Why
Why

For to us all you gave your son to die upon the cross.
You too understand sacrifice, pain, and loss.

Why
Why
Why

Hate and anger no more,
instead, forgiveness, hope, and love evermore.

Why
Why
Why

God's plan we may not always know,
but I am overjoyed of this gift to bestow.

Hope

Hope
It's a simple word
with so much power,
it's absurd.

It's a feeling of anticipation.
It's a desire, belief, or expectation.
It's God's promise and plan.
It's a wish for every man.

It's a symbol of love.
It's rainbows, olive branches, and a dove.
It's being optimistic, positive, and full of trust.
It keeps our focus on achieving goals a must.

It's **H**elping others,
our sisters and our brothers.
It's giving **O**thers support, strength, faith, and will.
It's providing **P**eople and parents the peace to chill.
It's giving the gift of **E**ndurance.

It's reminding us all of God's assurance.

HOPE

Kindness

Imagine a world where
everyone was kind.
Where examples of nice
were easy to find.

People were not quick
to judge.
Nobody held
a grudge.

Everyone took time
to listen.
To understand
another's position.

A world where there was
empathy for another.
Love and patience
for your sister and brother.

It is easy to scatter kindness
everywhere you go.
Then watch happiness grow.

Kindness breeds unity
and compassion.
Increasing positive interaction.

So, it's a simple solution,
Let's start a kindness revolution.

Just start today….

Be kind.
Pass it on.

Hummingbirds

A beautiful little bird
whose wings have
rapidly whirred.

As I sit and watch you
flitter in flight,
such an
aerodynamic delight.

With your forked tongue
and flexible beak,
seeking out your diet of insects,
sugar water,
and nectar is anything
but bleak.

Migrating from Alaska to Mexico,
each year we are sad to see you go.

Every spring we await
your return.
To hear the humming
of your wings and
watch your tiny
body hover
is what we yearn.

Dream

Dream big and large,
Dream of your goals,
take charge.

Dream of the past.
Dream of the present.
Dream of the future.

Dreams are made to follow.
Do not wallow.

Dream to keep memories
alive so they last.

Dream of loved ones
you hold dear.
Dream of places traveled
far and near.

Courage

What does having
courage mean?

Sometimes the need for it cannot be foreseen.

When your life is tuned upside down,
Courage is needed to keep you from a breakdown.

To face life's challenges head-on and brave.
Being able to face fears and others' betrayal forgave.

Now full of grit,
I will never quit.

Dare To Live

No matter the circumstances
or the pain,
You must live your life,
You have so much to gain.

Let your heart and
soul be free,
forgiving all is key.

Go out and enjoy.
Be a cowboy.

Do the dare.
Do it with flair.

Try something new and fun.
Your adventure has just begun.

Be brave, courageous, and strong,
Write your own theme song.

Make a bucket list to complete.
Don't stop until you've achieved your feat.

Forgiveness

"H" took you away,
Anger and hate needed to pay.

The proof was easy to find.
How could some be so blind?

Justice we tried to seek,
Though the outcome remained bleak.

A choice to be made,
Move on or remain full of hate.
I chose to let go and forgive,
I decided to live.

With hate and anger gone,
honoring you in writing,
was my focus from dusk to dawn.

With my soul free,
living for both you and me.

Forgiving another is a must,
not doing so causes
your life to combust.

To choose forgiveness,
makes your soul feel light,
and keeps the rest
of your days bright.

Peace

I close my eyes,
as I look to the skies.

I take a deep breathe in,
I can see your grin!

But when I exhale,
I'm taken back
to the night when,
I see your body cold and pale.

On your knees face down
and frail.
We can all still hear me wail.

A new life in the clouds,
you can now begin.
Your stress and anxiety can now cease.
My wish for you,
Peace.

My Angel

You are always with me,
Nobody can see.

I hear your voice in my head.
It's like you aren't even dead.

I know to others that
sounds insane.
What they do not know
is that our bond
will never wane.

So, what they think,
I do not care.
Because I know
our connection is rare.

My darling angel,
I miss you each day
you are not here.
I find comfort knowing
you are near.

Thanks….
My angel.

See You Again

When will I see you again?
I anticipate the moment;
I have visions of when
we will meet.

I see you standing next
to Jesus.
A huge smile upon your face,
I stand frozen in place.
I want to run, but I can't,
Tears of joy flow down my face.

There are flowers and sunshine all around.
I hear water trickling in the distance.
A light breeze blows my hair.
A beautiful scent is in the air.

Oh, how I have longed for this day to come!
Suddenly, startled out of
my trance by your
familiar voice,
"Mom," you say and reach out your hand.
I take a step,
One step turns into two,
then I'm running towards you!

I go to you first,
hoping Jesus will understand.
I run into your arms.
My heart is overpouring
with love.
Your hug is tight
like old times.

Your hands,
I love those hands.
Those dirty, cracked
little boy hands,
The ones I couldn't let go of,
as I held them cold
in the mortuary basement.
They are now warm and pulsing with love.

Oh, I love you, my son!
When I see you again!

Feathers All Around

Fluffy white plume
there in my path.

I know it's from my angel.
No need to assume.

Blessed to be shown he is near,
leaving feathers all around.

They come in many colors
white, brown, and yellow.
Sometimes I see them
on the ground.

Purple, black, and gray.
They appear without a sound.

Thank you, sweet angel,
for leaving feathers all around.

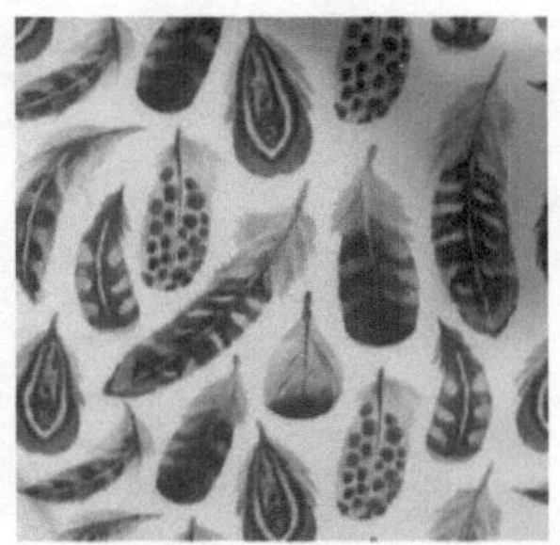

References

PsalmsQuotes.com

ABOUT THE AUTHOR

Angie was born in South Dakota and now resides in Stansbury Park, Utah with her husband Duane, daughter Kaylee, and two grand dogs Avery and Gracie. She loves adventure, trying new things, and being around people, especially children. She has spent her career as an elementary teacher, an elementary principal, and a secondary assistant principal.

She loves fashion, especially shoes and anything that sparkles. Her hobbies include shopping, decorating, reading, and traveling. The thing that is most important to her is spending time with her family.

Her first book, *Life Rolls On,* is one of honesty and strength. It's a tribute to her late son, Cody Gillette, who lost his battle with addiction at the age of 26. In it she shares her story to honor him and to help others understand the battle of addiction. Also, to let other parents and families know that they are not alone in this epidemic and that life can roll on, it may not be easy, but with kindness, understanding instead of judgment, and empathy toward others we can all learn to appreciate each other.

Angie has always enjoyed writing and teaching writing. However, writing has become a new passion of hers especially, writing from the heart. When she lost her son, it was a way to help her heal.

Dearest Readers,

I believe that writing is an art. Writing has always been a passion of mine. I have always loved to write and as a teacher, I loved to teach writing especially poetry. For me writing has played an instrumental part in my healing process after the loss of my son in 2018. Through writing, I can pour my heart out. While some thoughts and feelings being expressed may be dark, by getting them out on paper, I am able to release them in a sense and let them go. Others are full of hope, which bring me happiness and fill me with gratitude. I am including a few blank pages for you to take your turn at being a writer. I hope it is as healing and inspiring for you as it is for me.

Best Wishes.
Happy Writing!
Love,
Angie Gillette

It's Your Turn to be the Poet...

It's Your Turn to be the Poet...

It's Your Turn to be the Poet...

It's Your Turn to be the Poet...

It's Your Turn to be the Poet...

It's Your Turn to be the Poet...

www.ingramcontent.com/pod-product-compliance
Lightning Source LLC
LaVergne TN
LVHW090048160826
845672LV00015B/1603

* 9 7 9 8 7 2 5 9 8 0 6 8 4 *